ractive Press

om the Arctic

Libby Hart was a recipient of a D J O'Hearn Memorial Fellowship at The Australian Centre, University of Melbourne (2003). Her suite of poems, Fresh News from the Arctic, won the Somerset National Poetry Prize (2005).

Libby's poems have appeared widely in both Australian and overseas publications.

Fresh News from the Arctic *was Highly Commended in the 2006 IP Picks Best Poetry competition.*

The **Emerging Authors Series** *showcases the best Australian emerging literary talent and is available in digital and print form.*

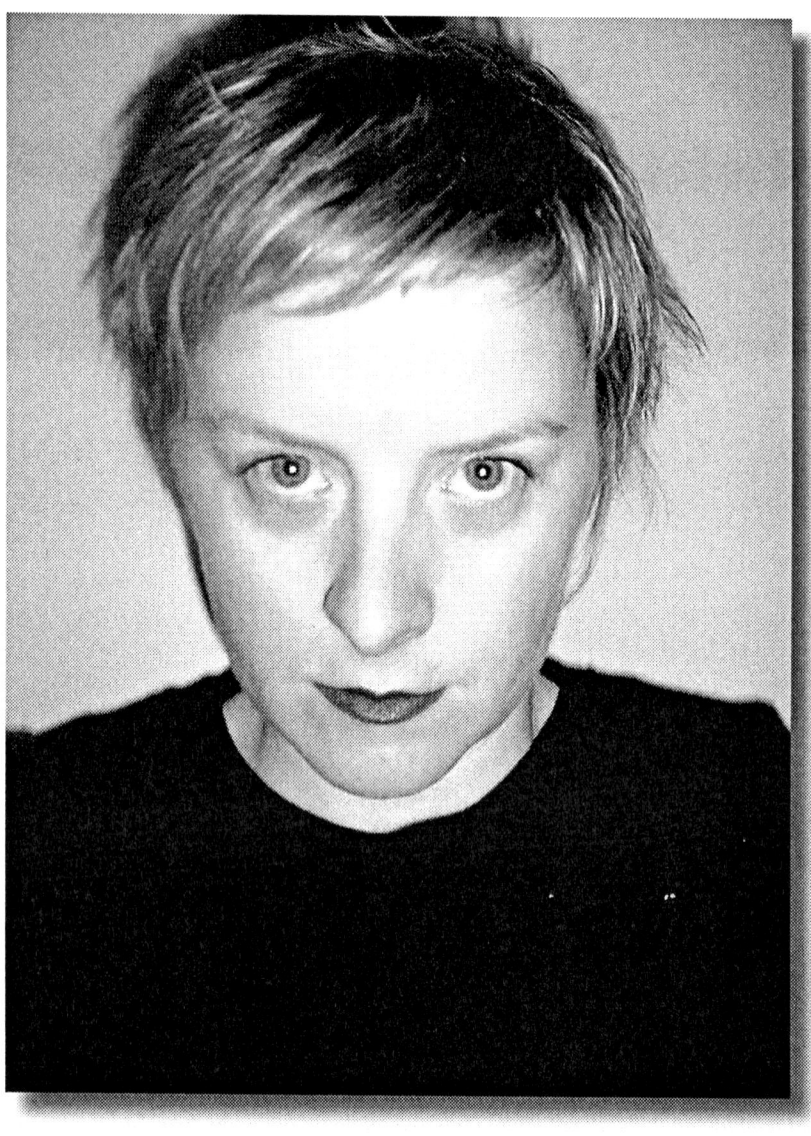

Fresh News from the Arctic

Libby Hart

Interactive Press
Brisbane

Interactive Press
an imprint of Interactive Publications
Treetop Studio • 9 Kuhler Court
Carindale, Queensland, Australia 4152
sales@ipoz.biz
www.ipoz.biz/ip/ip.htm

First published by Interactive Press, 2006
© Libby Hart, 2006
Lightning Source edition, 2007

All rights reserved. Without limiting the rights under copyright reserved above, no part of this publication may be reproduced, stored in or introduced into a retrieval system, or transmitted, in any form or by any means (electronic, mechanical, photocopying, recording or otherwise), without the prior written permission of the copyright owner and the publisher of this book.

Printed in 11 pt Cochin on 14 pt Trebuchet MS by by Lightning Source UK and USA.

National Library of Australia
Cataloguing-in-Publication data:

Hart, Libby, 1971- .
Fresh news from the Arctic.

ISBN 9781876819347.

ISBN 1 876819 34 0.

I. Title. (Series : Emerging authors).

A821.4

This project has been supported by the Commonwealth Government through the Australia Council, its arts funding and advisory body.

Acknowledgments

Jacket Design: David Reiter

Author Photos: Sophie McClusky

I gratefully acknowledge the editors of the publications in which these poems, some in earlier versions and with different titles, first appeared: *Sunweight: 2005 Newcastle Poetry Prize Anthology, The Sydney Morning Herald, Retort Magazine, Muse Magazine, Eureka Street Magazine, Poetrix, Voices in the Roses* (United Kingdom), *The Black Mountain Review* (Northern Ireland), *New England Review, BeeHive* (USA), *The Australian, Talvipaivanseisaus Specials* (Finland), *The Age, Divan, In Our Own Words: A Generation Defining Itself, Vol. 5* (USA).

"My Father is a Tumbleweed" was broadcast on *PoeticA*, ABC Radio National.

I am grateful to The Australian Centre (University of Melbourne) for a D J O'Hearn Memorial Fellowship. Sincere appreciation is extended to Kate Darian-Smith and Chris Wallace-Crabbe.

Contents

Fresh News from the Arctic	*1*
Planting a Weeping Birch	*9*
The Anatomy of Clouds	*10*
Tightrope Walker	*14*
Circumnavigation	*15*
Darwin's Walk	*16*
The Ghost of James Hegarty	*18*
Mist	*20*
Samuel Beckett's Wrinkles	*21*
Family on the Moon	*22*
Unfolding	*23*
Heirloom	*24*
The Memory Suite	*26*
Metamorphosis	*28*
The Dream Jar	*30*
Sylph	*31*
Coming Up for Air	*32*
Myopia	*33*
Room of Angels	*34*
Inventory	*35*
Venezia	*36*
In Development	*37*
My Father is a Tumbleweed	*38*
Between	*39*
Nicolas Baudin	*41*

The Japanese Wrap Things So Well	*47*
Concealment	*48*
Pigeonholes	*49*
The Briefcase Phenomenon	*50*
Inheritance	*51*
Pollen	*53*
Notes	*55*

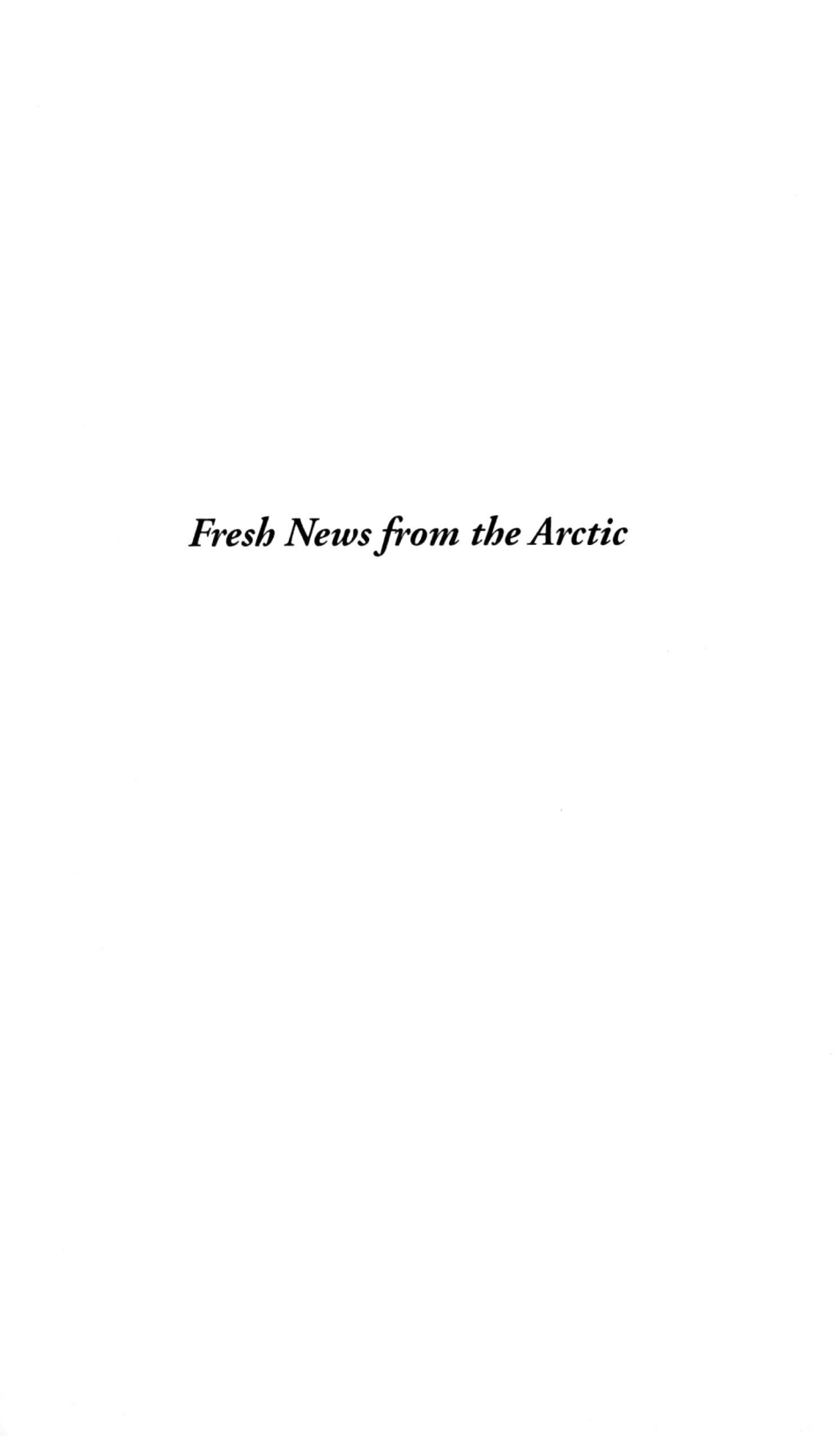

Fresh News from the Arctic

Fresh News from the Arctic

I.

Inside a dusky breath
I watched the edge of light,
radiant and graceful in its retreat.

I whispered: *Arctos*
and felt the ground beneath me fall.
I observed the swelling of the earth.

I was leaving the known, the traceable.
Heading out to climb the goal,
to swing and hitch the rope.

There is more to this than the surface.
I took a fancy
to your hills of little secrets

To the quilted ice, your lace of snow.
Seducer in blue
I repeated your name. *Arctos*.

Twisted the notion
of true north around my tongue.
I desired the taste of you.

At that distance
the earth looked like a changeling, a phantom spirit.
I conjured and I beckoned.

II.

When I arrived,
I moved as if to speak
but the birds were heavy
with their dialogue.

I left them to their bickering
and moved into the light.
The air was full of willow seed,
and as strange as possibility.

August, I thought, was a month of jewels.
Being speechless
became my new way.
I learnt how to culture the ear,

To hear nuance in the landscape.
Sound overshadowed all other senses.
Precise and complete, I listened
to the crackle of a short autumn,

To creeping ice, and shivering poppies
squat against the earth.
I lent my eyes to white ferocity,
retreated from touch and taste.

My sense of smell tightly froze
while I listened to the approaching snow
deepening its resolve,
becoming graceful constellations.

III.

For the first time in my life, the cold bothers me.
This would seem rather an obvious statement,
but I've lived my life like Gabriel,
swooning over the *faintly falling* snow.

It's the progression of loneliness that ices my way.
There's a pattern, a routine that's followed through.
I've crept into a self-imposed exile,
only to realise that my bones are built differently.

IV.

This is where winter shapes itself.

More hut than a snow igloo,
it's a breezy contraption
anchored at hillside.

Ice wreckage
looped by whalebone and skin.
Too like a ghost
to feel comfortable inside
its thick walls.

I've been thinking of spirit photography,
of the apparition at my shoulder
fading into paper.

The thought of you remains.

V.

When the sun falls low
dipping to a curved steer,
my heart becomes a heavy stone.

I acknowledge the darkness
like a black seed, which has chosen me
and is nurturing a foreboding.

Dark reverberations
of the people who've inhabited this house.
Interlinked misadventurers

Pushing fingerprints into walls,
that then incline into journeys.
They've fallen a long way

From the expectations of a new life,
grizzled Poes who've buried bones
under floorboards.

I stretch my hands out,
rub them back and forth
to rekindle touch.

I hear the years of vacant possession,
the poetics of empty space,
of the dust settling.

I'm not sure
if I'm the haunted
or if I'm doing the haunting.

VI.

I breathe a London fog of fine concoction.
Like Captain Walton, I'm listening
to the slow shattering of my life.

I daydream about leaving
yet something keeps me here,
keeps me tied to the distance.

Every shade of white,
every variation of sorrow.
The wind buries my footprints.
I wait.
I wait.
I'm hoping for inner resolution.

It must come like a mast, like a sail;
with an almighty north wind,
prodigious and impressive.

I'm trying to read
the sky for confirmation.
Diamond dust, swirling.

Falling over me. Into me.

VII.

Sometimes I can take the beauty in
and hold it there –

The tapestry of *aurora borealis*,
the boom-crash of pack ice,
an arctic fox deep in mischief-making.

I'm in love
with the awkward feet of reindeer.

I'm perpetually suited to the *idea* of this land –
only my mind has other plans.
In every sense, I see this as my failing.

I dream of boat-building.
I'm left with a clear blueprint,

A misshapen vessel
constructed by somnambulism –
buoyant and eager for departure.
An *umiak*,
it slips away as I wake.

VIII.

If *white* were a colourful word
I'd have to strip it down to this –
pale, washed out. An absence of energy
except for the gradation. But isn't life about shade?
Isn't it the shadows that make life interesting?

My mind wanders
over clouds that are blue and grey,
stippled by the ocean.
I feel alive today.

I'm somewhere, nestled
between good fortune and hope.
I've struck a deal with change.
I'm motioning,
becoming arched and bound.

This is the voyage out.
I'm leaving. Just like that.
I've packed my instincts like a trio of golden birds;
becoming a tidal chart, I'm calculated to the second.

I've dowsed the burning letters, removed the clumsy furniture,
and turned things inside and out. There's no longer
a place for everything and everything in its place.
I'm living like a tight wire.
I'm mesmerising animals, I'm seeking embers.

I've stripped the bones bare, and
bleached them for authenticity.
I've left the air fresh with expectation.
My dogs are restless and keen to make a start.

IX.

I whisper: *Arctos*
and listen to the wet slap of an oar
shape the rhythm of the journey.

I have a talisman.
It comes in the form of a grey seal
who is ever watchful,

Circling, and disappearing into the calm water.
Reappearing with wide yawns
and a strange tongue.

A tiger moth swoops low,
a fiery phoenix, it burns a patch of sky.
I follow earnestly

Edging my way toward the timberline,
remembering that it's better to travel
hopefully than to arrive safely.

I'm straightening my boomerang
as I repeat your name. *Arctos*.
There is more to this than the surface.

More to this than your *blue meadow* of icebergs,
to the outline of narwhal, the grim dentistry of walrus.
More than the palpitation of evening lights on the main land,

Or a sea otter, anchored by seaweed while it sleeps.
Everything feels new, but my heart is old.
Moth-like, I reach out to oncoming traffic.

Night rain becomes its own vigil,
curved by arterial stars –
all vivid and misguided.

I reach for the silhouetted trees,
for the touch of bark and leaves.

Planting a Weeping Birch

In its drought skin
the earth is hard to peel,
to split open into a wound.

He uses his entire body
its sinewy muscles
to become one tool of digging

One rhythm with many punches.
The ground quivers
into panic, and

His determination self-seeds
in the humid air
like Campion weed,

The shovel becoming prosthesis
as he digs and digs,
hard-edged into ground

Now swollen by blows
and no longer resisting the tree,
but holding it in its skin

Unsure of its embrace,
yet allowing it to wind its way
through the heart of new terrain.

The Anatomy of Clouds

Altostratus, 1912

She: containing the swell of her
He: the soft vowels of Athenry

the damned or the mighty
in their Sunday clothes

Her home: a room, an idea of marriage, a coat hook
He: a stranger in this part of town

removes his dog collar
before taking the steps to her room.

She: like a bird hiding itself in cloud
He: like soft, patient rain

this, being the ocean of air in which they live

one knowing it would last
the other, believing in a promise of something more

as he moves from one world to another
with a sense of belonging but not belonging.

Cirrus, 1910

Just blossom and exist, he said
so I stretched out across the wild blue
and beyond the sea

becoming shapeless and delicate
drifting along the light breezes

   a tuft of blossom
      inside a wild garden of air

Nimbostratus, 1911

We are clouds.

Moving and abating
breathing in the wind

measuring condensation

collecting its persistency
until it glistens on our backs.

Buried deep is the nimbus

that holds us together
a suspended water, bulking.

The softest kind of rain

that lasts all through the day
making a street slick in the wake of it

until it crackles with promise

against a black umbrella –
a multitude of bat wings vaulted.

The air is still now. We only know

a delicacy of vapours,
an infinity of revelation.

Cumulonimbus, 1913

A storm takes a long time to build
(sometimes it even takes a lifetime)

all its seams and tangles become
a song, a thread unfolding

dark and blown away
its chiaroscuro forming all the words for *moody*,

the sky pressuring into rain.
A shape-shifter from way back

it's too grief-stricken to know anything of routine,
instead it clings to the form of ideas

to the wool bags that fall heavily at its knees.
You once said that you saw yourself

in the energy that strains and boils, and
I remember how you grew overcast

shadows blooming to great height,
your cold front meeting my warm front like hailstorm.

My heart closed itself within itself
as a form of preservation

binding our secrets in layers
until I am all but an onion, wrapped tight.

The midwife urges me to push
as a ribbon of light divides the sky, and

into the woods comes whalesong
the sea, lapping in a gale force

underneath the soil of things,
all shipwrecked and wretched.

I feel the swell of my belly,
sense the moving child within
pushing his way through me.
He's determined to arrive.

I say, here are my pearls of breath
here are my hands.

Even in the harshest storm
I will shelter you.

Tightrope Walker

She walks the sky
with mathematical precision

travels lightly
freedom nesting in her hair.

Life begins at this altitude
with the rush of verve through the heart.

When the crowd becomes a sea of eyes
she thinks of Alice

    falling toward a new kingdom.

Circumnavigation

His hand moves roundly,
looping distance.
A quick and assured gap of life
on a wide sheet of paper.

He measures the rises and the contours.
Pen at the ready, finding momentum
like a wheel. Tangling the air.
Defining travelled steps.

The scratch of a pen becomes a guided tour,
carrying him to a plump line of thought
of soft, falling desires –

Of a special curve to conquer,
a night train to fall asleep in.
A bed that is unmade, yet inviting.

Darwin's Walk

Nobody traipses anymore.
No one lingers over a spot
thinking for 20 years about origins or earthworms,
no one bothers to clock up over 20,000 circuits
contemplating the world.

Each grain of sand, a time capsule
mulled over now by gravel for tourists
who stay awhile
and walk the bended edges of Darwin's imaginings,
just past the kitchen garden and the meadow.

I think imagination needs to be curved.
It has to be full and rounded.
There's no point in narrowness,
it is thin-aired and has its limits.

Bending carries laterality
and room for improvement,
an endless cycle of preoccupation.
Circles are for dreamers

Straight lines, on the other hand
are for middle men
for men in suits,
for bitter wives.

Einstein's *Theory of Relativity* seems doomed for revision
but Darwin's theory still stands up, more or less
160 years after telling his wife to open
the bundle of papers in the event of his death,
binding its shame in ribbon.

Containing it like a toxic secret
until its guilty knowledge flowered from competition,

allowing polite women to utter the word *ape*
for the first time in relation to ourselves,
speaking in whispers so as not to upset the servants.

Hierarchies climb and crumble like radiation
each set of rules or animal
replaced by another, and another
like time and the notion of substance.

Walking each day
step after step,
one foot in front of the other.
Murmuring the world,
grasping it slowly.

The Ghost of James Hegarty

I've come early to this house.

I return, you see.
Just like you.

I set myself down by the edge of your bed

to touch the feet that lie there.
I know you want to ask it.

But no, I never did see her mother grow tall.

As silent as the moon, we carried tide through vein
salt water in blood

We were vessels for an ocean.

On land our eyes searched for liquid.
We looked for a neat frame, a pleasant view of coast

to become our anchor.

We were islanders
borderless, we understood the sum

the totality of completeness.

Our minds comprehended mobility
and our feet balance

while we learnt to carry that island on our backs.

Like turtles, we moved slowly through the day
on a ship as wide as the earth.

Crowded, we all held fast to dreams

and drank rain heavy with tears.
Sipped it gently in reticence.

Our thoughts focused on the Tuatha de Danaan

in their long curraghs skimming waves
to reach Ireland's western shore

only to set fire to their boats.

There was no turning back,
and we repeated that ancient story

as we burnt

mythical ships
in the harbour of our dreams.

Memories rushed through our blood

with each heartbeat,
and held rain and snow within.

We sang love songs to mist, to craggy shores.

We dreamt of the Irish Sea
with letters wrapped tightly in seaweed.

I know you want to ask it.

But no, I never did see her mother grow tall
and she never sensed my instep beside her.

Mist

Building into night
we construct
a hidden language

a block of time
that shapes a sweet music.

Like the blind
we go in search of fingertips
or the feel of wet grass under foot.

We breathe stars
into mist.

Samuel Beckett's Wrinkles

It starts with an untidy map
held within skin,
deep and heavy on the head

And becomes an avenue of *this*, a river of *that*
a crossroad, meeting between eyebrow
curved and bent beyond recognition;

A roundabout
at cheek and chin,
drawing the mouth into recess.

Eyes are unexplored terrain
while hair, always neater than the face,
reaches for sky.

Family on the Moon

The world rotated
at the click of the camera

So smoothly did it turn
we remained steady on our feet
roaming our paths of destiny.

Captured, we now live with youthful smiles
polished skin and tidy hair.
Neck ties, shaped wide and stiff.

A bright shirt
a vision of red, resting strangely against the landscape.

As a snapshot
we have come to visit
but find no one home.

A message of our oddity – thin legs and arms
greet the moon's surface.

If you should come across this neat photograph
look for us out across the darkness.

We belong to the blue world.
We depend on the moon for company.
The stars are our loneliness, the sun our meaning.

Unfolding

Take my hand
and I will open, palm up

as if I were a magnolia flower,
entirely in curvature.

Falling out of myself
knuckle after knuckle.

In a sense, escapology
the allure of carnival trick.

Heirloom

My grandmother's hands
were like warm cups of milky tea
made from the best china.

When we drove into town
she'd grip the dashboard like a skydiver
waiting for her parachute to open.
My mother said she was always like this about cars

but I've noticed how in photographs
she'd clutch a bare arm of a daughter or her glasses
and sensing her hesitation
I see how the influence of cancer worked through
her confidence, as well as through her soft body.

Before this
she'd put on her thick stockings
and clipping them into suspenders
she'd jump from the bed
to tidy her dress with a firm hand

in the backyard
where the smell of perfume lingered
she'd stand with the sun at her back
placing clothes on the line,
a polyester dress shushing the air as she moved.

But cancer knows patience
and creates a carapace while it lingers,
where once there was only blood and soft tissue
under the hood of skin.

I remember, on holidays
how I'd help her with the shopping
and we'd march through Myer and into Safeway
breathlessly buying jelly babies for my uncle
and two fruits and ice cream for her guests, and

returning to the car
we'd find my grandfather at the steering wheel
scribbling through a cryptic crossword,
and as he looked up he'd move toward small talk.

And when the car shook itself into reverse
her hands were always
fixed in the direction of home.

The Memory Suite

Old teapot

Warm to the touch
it holds itself like a small fire

I like to wrap my fingers around it
hold its heat inside palm –
its calmness, growing darker with each hour.

Washday

A mountain of washing
one week long
stands on the cold floor.
I call it *Himalayas*
explore its territory
hour by hour
scrub it clean of fault
then
hang its geography
piece by piece
out to dry.

Air raid shelter

The colour comes to me
before anything else:
charcoal, near blindness.

Sirens call us away
from our warm beds
from a sense of security
held only in dreams.

Inside this cave
darkness holds each wall in suspension
like hands around the neck.

Hospital

The gentle nurse
has plumped my pillows
tucked me tighter into this steely bed

I am asked not to move

I reassure myself in the comfort of bandages
the unusual pleasure of the doctor's cool, clean hands
his lightest touch of thumb, and then finger, at the wrist.

Metamorphosis

Her heart blossoms
moving into the old ways
hair extending into golden tresses
to abscond from the neckline.

Invisible fingers clip each strand into place
building a golden breath of light –
an unearthly choreography
powdering and colouring the cheek
then tightening corsetry (a breath collapses).

She stands obediently
as they gently lift her bosom
encasing it within a sky-blue dress that billows
leaving the skin to tingle.

Marvellous and strange
sensation fills her body whole
a great brunt of feeling, of masked excitement
shaping itself and drawing feet into slippers –
a fine brocade at the edge of freshly mown lawn.

Her complexion, smoothing and paling in its alteration
is all baroque and incandescent, and bathed
in cumbersome beauty. Like a dream
the scent of violets.

The garden collapses, shimmering into fragments
a large oak rising from the earth fully-formed
to build a blueprint of foliage by her feet.
A hand gathers its new leaves, each
a cold-soft touch like the first stroke of kid gloves.

And then, a row of linden tree and an avenue of gravel
a lush wall of Irish yew, and roses
falling to bloom, all drunken and tiptoed –
petals scatter haphazardly.

A swarm of bees carries the fragrance of the afternoon.
Ever watchful, she waits
for this moment to falter like heaven
as rain spreads its hand lightly over such luminosity.
In a word: enchantment (a breath, a sigh).

The Dream Jar

This jar made of glass and heavy with cloud
throbs to the touch
like a deer I have startled it.
Heartbeats press into the palm of my hand.

I watch it as if it were a film
keep an eye on its clouds
see how a forest of them turns sharply into sky
then into portraits
which hang deep inside cumulus form.

Actions occur in silence
a tight lid holds conversations well
but there isn't much to tell –
words are just air with meanings.

Untouchable syllables
ooze through skin, sentences pass into fingerprints.
Rain begins to fall.

I see my dream of snails inside each drop of rain –
one million snails in the garden.
With the morning light approaching
I stand with bare feet on the path
as they ride my toes as hills.

Sylph

From lung root,
a quick breath
hauling oxygen

to carry you
through a corridor of trees.
Formation of night, hovering.

You *are* the wind –
both faithful and faithless.

Landing, and overstepping the mark
tender feet fall
on Prospero's open books,
scattered in a slant of light.

Walking their black text
breathing in magic,
acknowledging something known and traceable.

This is the trade entering your body.

Coming Up for Air

Breaking the news into several pieces.
   Cutting it loose,
      all strings and ties, and bows and arrows.

      Filling my arms with air.
   Returning for seconds,
spreading the world thin.

Taking gravity
   like a slice of pie.
      Stealing it blind.

      Honouring the fallen
   while the birches weep.
Shattering the glass of silence.

Coming up for air
   along a smooth edge of river.
      Pressing the point until I find a button.

Myopia

I.

If I crawl my way toward you
you will know that I cannot see clearly
without the aid of a small distance.

II.

If I walk through mirrors
I become the shape of something new
something familiar.

III.

If I were to read your eyes as Bibles
I would find a message in there
somewhere.

Room of Angels

We are identical,
yet different.

Defined by wing,
a set of white heat and duck feathers.

We speak in tongues,
we speak with our tongues

Inside an enclosed room.
So small is this room

Our wings are clipped.
Pushed back against spine.

Restless, we ruffle easily.
We speak in tongues.

Our criterion is our uniform.
Only our faces recognise our faces.

Inventory

Long eyelashes
    and short fringes

for boys
    in school uniform

who gather
    like scuttled animals

restless
    inside leather shoes.

Venezia

I could easily live in a gondola,
but I'd need a roof
and plump cushions to lounge on
as I slipped through the night
with the boatman's call hugging at my chest.

I could easily live in a gondola,
but I'd need dry days
where the water was as still as the earth
and I'd glide patiently across its glassy surface
with the thought of hope pinching at my toes.

I could easily live in a gondola,
but I'd need a full dress of silk
with a whalebone corset
pulled tightly enough for hallucinations
that would come to me like arrows

The world dancing across the jaggedness of tide
and I'd feel the essence of it, like a Zen monk
completing the circle in Indian ink, and
the night would swallow the earth
with its inky shadow.

In Development

This has somehow
become a clandestine affair
that burns holes through nightfall

Yet as hot and heavy as this may sound
there's still the freezing of trees
that snap clean
against a hard edge
of a lonely road,
slicing the gutter up
with useless timber.

But even in the wintering
I am able to recognise your form,
to watch its shifting shape
as it transgresses.

And I've decided that it's you I have faith in,
more so than what measurement I can give.
It's you, who stops on the edge of thought
while I rummage through restlessness.
It's you, who is growing determined,
who is learning to speak your mind.

My Father is a Tumbleweed

Tall and slim in circus shapes
he took his time
to slip into shadow

it began with dreams
of a freeway's unbroken line

then quietly
he divided, cell into cell into cell
becoming wind and dust
rattling inside a tangled lair.

Between

Tolstoy walked out into the snow.
Chekhov may or may not have had champagne.
Sylvia Plath neatly folded a dishcloth in the oven for her head.
Tchaikovsky tried drowning himself, only to stand hip deep
    in the Moskva River.
Shelley was more successful, heading straight into a storm
    with a copy of Keats in his pocket.
Miklós Radnóti buried his poems in his pocket before someone
    buried him.
Virginia Woolf had faith in the rock that held her down in
    The Ouse.

※　※　※

In the silence,
the car has already turned for Sebald
the cancer already taken Brodsky
the ocean already swallowed Hart Crane.

In suffering,
Rimbaud nurses his bad leg
Jane Austen reflects on her illness
Mary Wollstonecraft insists on bravery.

In the darkness,
Henry James writes invisible words over a bedspread
Keats undergoes his long final nights
Eugene O'Neill waits to die in a Boston hotel room.

In rapidity,
Pushkin falls from the bullet
Marlowe bleeds in Deptford
Hemingway places the gun to his head
while the Brontës drop away
   like pearls from a broken necklace.

Nicolas Baudin

I.

The heart holds its own knowledge
like a time capsule.
It is sentient

and ill-equipped to renounce information,
yet not quite accustomed to living with it either.
It holds all of it tightly, unable to let go.

My advice is to
ignore the beating.
Ignore the incessant drumming

that dances near the ribcage.
Ignore this.
Listen to its quieter language

its murmuring in the blood,
surrounding the body
with experience.

There are scars here,
unseen and minute –
too small for the human eye.

Bring a microscope.
Step up to it.
Look closer.

Do you see them?
Do you hear it
lulling him toward sleep?

A siren
belting out a memory
or a glimpse of *famille*.

II.

In the half light
he acknowledges
the outline of a kangaroo.

He already knows she's there
beside him,
her belly expanding

and contracting
with the shallow breath
of someone who is dying.

If she were allowed counsel
she'd confide that
not having found her sea legs

she was never meant for the water,
was never meant to find peace
over the collapsible world

where she now finds herself.
It is almost too arduous
to take in

concern
blooming across her brow, but
the intention of the Frenchman

who soothes her with small kindness
is comprehensive. He makes it clear
that it is all right, they are *all* dying.

Sickness brings affiliation,
benevolence
a measure of dependency.

III.

Outside
the men hold their criticism
under fingernails, and

he thinks
their eyes are as sharp as daggers,
but here, inside this small cabin

the air is thick-scented
by seven kangaroos
who are as quiet as folded hands.

True originals
from the southern hemisphere
destined for the Empress,

for her *collection of pure pleasure*.
And they are more real to him than anything.
More true, more faithful

than any animal he has known.
Is it not understandable that
to look into the eyes of a kangaroo

is to feel real warmth?
Let the heart take this experience
and lock it in.

IV.

Somewhere
in the immensity
that is the Indian Ocean

a man learns patience
and his thoughts begin to hover
like cumulus cloud.

When his lungs
no longer desire
to remain in his body

he holds the jar firmly
and convulses.
His heart remembers this.

V.

If Baudin had survived this journey
he would've known
that seven minus five equals

two kangaroos
arrived safely in Paris.
But he doesn't.

Instead
his body is placed
in a hasty coffin, and

dug deep
inside a snug anchor
of forgetfulness.

And while
the revisionists worked
on their fictions

of disproportion
the kangaroos
grew accustomed

to the landscape
at Malmaison
and became

the very embodiment
of relaxation –
their soft mouths

crunching time away
as they lazed on their sides
like misshapen and ancient stones.

VI.

Today
wild kangaroos
can be found

in the Rambouillet Forest,
happily existing
just outside the town of Emance.

Generations of escapees
who fled a French animal park
thirty years prior.

Josephine
would've been pleased
to have a legacy

so close to Paris
but, more importantly,
Baudin would be delighted

the edges of his mouth
curling into a small boat
at the very thought of it; and

at the obstinate nature
of the *peaceful creatures*
who don't complain.

The Japanese Wrap Things So Well

Hidden
is my heart
in seven layers

like the skin
of my body
wrapped tightly
in indigo paper

fibre of linen
gentle silk
and tied with vine

Concealment

She binds herself together
strapping her feet into Chinese proportions,
curving her back to resemble stone.

And gift-wrapped by snow
she lapses into concealment,
knowing the worst has passed *or* is yet to pass.

Her breath taking on its own life
becoming looped curlicues of tangled whispers,
dancing with twilight time.

All is stone; an encasement.
Nothing short of turtle or beetle.
Unbreakable.

Breathing in and out.
Steady now. Steady.
Remembering the horses in the meadow.

Remembering them.
Their smell, their lovely speed.
The look on their faces.

The night gallops away.

Pigeonholes

Mostly, you see what you want to see – eclipse or moonshine
nothing microscopic nor significant

just one million pigeonholes
hovering as if they were stars built into sky

held within opposites
contained by quote or exaggeration.

Name-calling becomes a majestic storm
circling the seams of life –

unpicking one stitch at a time.
My life opens up like a flower.

I'm laid bare against nature.
Girdled by curves

in tulip form
I carry a heaviness about me.

I've somehow been set-up
to waddle through my days

yet my true form
would best resemble the cherry blossom

suspended upon a ballooning sky –
to rise and fall on the tip of a calligrapher's pen.

The Briefcase Phenomenon.

An observation:
half-empty briefcases
(with apples rolling from side to side)
act as umbilical cords to the office.
A tidy mobile desk drawer with lid –
lockable, and weathered at the edges.

They do not leave the lap
and do not slide from side to side
but sit regally and flat-chested.

Just before the train delivers them home
men return their books into imitation leather
and sit impatiently like small children at home-time.

(It's like a private club
   or a ballet without music).

Inheritance

Maybe Samuel Beckett was right,
maybe the *tears of the world* exist
as a silent relay, circling the earth.

I impart.
My next door neighbour follows,
wearing her tears like jewellery.
They are large, misshapen pearls

And like the ancient Greeks
she'll collect them –
each and every one of them,
to bury them deep inside herself.

Each time is different:
small and barely noticeable
pooled at the lid –
blinking, blinking to remove

Or a heavy stream flowing
along the bridge of nose,
crossing the lips
circling, becoming a slick of salt.

And the relay expands into kilometres
through states and borders,
onto atolls and bridges
and dry land.

And, again, there is someone
who will follow the line,
who is picked for the flood.
An inheritor, with an urgency for tears.

Pollen

After the bruising
the pollen flowed

covering houses
and staining them yellow

as if the colour yellow
was an optimistic sign

for turning corners,
for brighter futures

and I was reminded
of the feather pattern of a hummingbird

of its soft leopard-like spots
woven into a cover of green, and

with this image,
I conjured up all the gleaners

spilling pollen
and doing their rounds, and

I watched them for a while
as I walked a street of miniature suns.

Notes

Fresh News from the Arctic

Arctos: Greek derivation for *Arctic*, meaning bear.

Gabriel and the faintly falling snow: 'The snow falling faintly through the universe, and faintly falling, like the descent of their last end, upon all the living and the dead.' (Joyce, J. "The Dead", *Dubliners*, Panther Books, London, 1977, p.201)

Captain Walton: the letter-writing narrator of *Frankenstein* by Mary Shelley.

Every variation of sorrow: Moody, R. *The Black Veil: A memoir with digressions*, Little Brown, New York, 2002, p.5.

Umiak: an Inuit boat, used by women to carry family belongings.

Blue meadow: a traditional Norwegian description of the sea.

The Anatomy of Clouds

The ocean of air in which they live: refers to Luke Howard's essay, "On the Modification of Clouds" where he describes the sky as being 'the ocean of air in which we live and move'.

Just blossom and exist: refers to a line from a letter written by Robert Louis Stevenson to Henry James.

The delicacy of these vapours: refers to a description by John Ruskin in *Modern Painters* in which he discusses the cirrus cloud.

The Ghost of James Hegarty

According to Irish Legend, the Tuatha De Danaan originated from the northern islands and immigrated to Ireland long ago in a great fleet of ships. On their arrival they set fire to their boats as a gesture of total commitment to the future and to their new life.

Family on the Moon

Family on the Moon was inspired by Charles Duke's gesture of leaving a family photograph on the moon's Descartes Highlands as a memento of his time on Apollo 16 in April 1972.

The Memory Suite

The Memory Suite refers to a story in *The Age* newspaper highlighting a nostalgia pack of smells designed by British psychiatrists to remind people of London during The Blitz. This pack was created to treat depression and memory loss. The scents included 'old teapot', 'washday', 'air raid shelter' and 'hospital'.

Recent IP Poetry

Imagining Winter, Paul Dawson
ISBN 9781876819361, AU$24

The Accidental Cage, Michelle Cahill
ISBN 9781876819392, AU$24

Dark Husk of Beauty, Andrew Leggett
ISBN 9781876819385, AU$24

3rd i, Basil Eliades
ISBN 9781876819323, AU$24

The possibility of winds, Rosemary Huisman
ISBN 9781876819330, AU$24

Subterranean Radio Songs, Joel Deane
ISBN 1876819316, AU$23

On Reflection, David Musgrave
ISBN 187681971X, AU$23

Popular Mechanics, Liam Ferney
ISBN 1876819219, AU$23

Joyflight, Cate Kennedy
ISBN 187681926X, AU$23

Café Boogie, Jenni Nixon
ISBN 187681926X, AU$23

For the latest from IP, please visit us online at
www.ipoz.biz/store/store.htm or sales@ipoz.biz
or contact us by phone on 61 7 3122 1312 or 61 7 3395 0269
by fax on 61 7 3324 9319

Title: *The Accidental Cage*
Author: Michelle Cahill
Publisher/Imprint: IP/Interactive Press
ISBN 10: 1-876819-39-1 • **ISBN 13:** 978876819392, PB, 72 pp. RRP: AU$24
Release Date: September 15, 2006

Description: Winner, Best First Book, IP Picks 2006. The Accidental Cage explores the perceptual and emotional experience of entrapment in its many forms. Exile, asylum, desire, love and motherhood all enter the speaker's imagination, often transformed by the force of resistance. The poems are nuanced, balancing a dramatic tension between the beauty of the metaphor and the impact of the meaning. The collection compiles longer meditations with shorter lyrical and imagistic poetry.

About the Author: Michelle Cahill's poems and reviews have appeared in journals such as *Callaloo, Going Down Swinging,* Journal of Australian Studies, *Cordite, Urthona* (UK), *Blue Dog, Verandah, Ulitarra, Imago, 4W, Poetrix, Vernacular,* and *Meusepress*. With a Creative Writing Arts Major from Macquarie University (1999), Michelle attended the Bread Loaf Writers' Conference in Vermont and the Catskill Poetry Conference in New York in 2004. One of three poets selected to tour southern NSW for the 2005 Poets On Wheels, she also received a scholarship from the Poetry Australia Foundation for its 2006 Poetry Workshop. She works as a part-time general practitioner in Sydney where she lives with her husband, David, and daughter, Tegan.

Michelle Cahill

Link: http://www.ipoz.biz/titles/ac.htm

Title: *The Possibility of Winds*
Author: Rosemary Huisman
Publisher/Imprint: IP/Interactive Press
ISBN: 978-1-876819-33-0
PB, 72pp. RRP: AU$24
Release Date: 1 June 2006

Description: Commended, IP Picks 2006, Best Poetry. "This is a world wonderfully changed by Rosemary Huisman's fine observation, playful intelligence and true feeling. Her poetry gives us what we need: it helps us recognize ourselves even as it constantly surprises us. A pleasure to read – and read again." – Noel Rowe
Rosemary's Huisman's first collection of poetry is an eclectic mix of the real world and typifies Rosemary's talent for paying attention to her surroundings and using it as an inspiration for her poetry. The poems in this collection touch on natural, social and political surroundings, as well as being particularly aware of language used by other people. These things combined make for an enjoyable and interesting read.

About the Author: Rosemary Huisman retired from the University of Sydney in 2003, where she is now an Honorary Associate Professor to the Department of English. She has published poems in Southerly, The Bulletin, and the Sydney Morning Herald. Her many academic publications include The Written Poem, Semiotic Conventions from Old to Modern English (London & New York, hb 1998 and pb 2000) and six chapters in Narrative and Media, with Helen Fulton, Julian Murphet and Anne Dunn (Cambridge, 2005).

Rosemary Huisman

Link: http://www.ipoz.biz/titles/TPW.htm

Title: *Hemingway in Spain*
Author: David Reiter
Publisher/Imprint: IP/IP.Digital
ISBN: 978-1-876819-86-6 DVD, 125 mins
RRP: AU$40
Release Date: 1 June 2006

Description: Borne out of the award-winning book of the same name, the *Hemingway In Spain* DVD is a visual and aural delight that takes the viewer on Hemingway's journey through Spain. Driven by readings from the key narrative poems, the DVD is a multimedia trip brought alive with Reiter's reading of related poems. The filmic aspects of the DVD, blending audio, stills and animation, follows Hemingway on his travel back in time on a quest for his arch-enemy Franco, during the Spanish Civil War. Along with his dream woman Maria, Hemingway also meets famous people from the past and future who have shocking things to say on war, love and art.

About the Author: David Reiter is the award-winning author of poetry, short story collections and novels. As well as being a pioneer in the digital arena of publishing, Dr Reiter is the director of Interactive Publications, a renowned Queensland publisher.

Link: http://www.ipoz.biz/titles/his-dvd.htm

David Reiter

Title: *Imagining Winter*
Author: Paul Dawson
Publisher/Imprint: IP/Interactive Press
ISBN 10: 1-876819-36-7 • ISBN 13: 9781876819361
PB, 88 pp. RRP: AU$24
Release Date: September 15, 2006

Description: Winner, Best Poetry, IP Picks 2006. The poems in *Imagining Winter* investigate contemporary urban existence, including the politics of national identity and the culture of inner city life in Sydney, Melbourne and Brisbane. Each of the three sections considers a different perspective of metropolitan landscapes and relationships. Poems within the first section, *Explorations*, manifest a reflexive awareness of the genre or of the process of writing itself: poems animated by an interest in form as much as subject. The second section, *Assertions*, includes declarative poems which deliver a political point or social commentary. Poems in the third section, *Preoccupations*, mirror more personal emotions, and ponder the nature of human relations.

About the Author: Paul Dawson's poetry and fiction have previously appeared in a range of literary journals and newspapers, including *Slope* (US), *Southerly, Blue Dog: Australian Poetry, Meanjin, Island, Imago: New Writing,* and *The Sydney Morning Herald*. He is also the author of *Creative Writing and the New Humanities* (London/New York: Routledge, 2005). He is now a Senior Lecturer in the School of English at the University of New South Wales, where he teaches Creative Writing and literary studies.

Paul Dawson

Link: http://www.ipoz.biz/titles/iw.htm

Title: *Joyflight*
Author: Cate Kennedy
Publisher/Imprint: IP/Interactive Press
ISBN: 1-876819-26 X 72pp. RRP: AU$23

Description: *Joyflight* is a collection of poems cleverly designed to 'shock a tiny gentleness from us' ("Five Encounters With Birds"). Cate Kennedy expresses endless sensitivity to the environment, to animals of all sizes, and to the past. Her poems portray a contemporary feminine outlook as in 'Potions' ('We fall for it every time, us second-wave women.') counterbalanced by an earthy rural sensibility. The collection is divided into two parts: **Part 1, That Pure Torn-Open Moment**, describes detailed observations of important personal moments; while **Part 2, Burning The World's Almanac**, focuses more on the Irish heritage observed by the author in a 2002 overseas visit.

About the Author: Cate Kennedy creates such an easy intimacy between author and reader that she could be mistaken for 'the girl next door'. In some ways she is, living on a farm on the Broken River in northeast Victoria. But Cate is also a multi-award winning poet, writer and lecturer. Her first published poetry collection *Signs of Other Fires* (Five Islands Press 2001) was Highly Commended in the **Victorian Premier's Awards**. In 2002, Cate won the **Vincent Buckley Poetry Award** making it possible for her to travel to Ireland where many of her *Joyflight* poems were conceived or written.

Cate Kennedy

Link: http://www.ipoz.biz/titles/jf.htm

Title: Kiss and Tell: Selected and New Poems, 1987-2002
Author: David P Reiter
Publisher/Imprint: IP/Interactive Press
ISBN: 1-876819-10-3 316pp. RRP: AU$25

Description: This selected and new is from one of Australia's most respected poets. Winner of the Queensland Premier's Award for Poetry and runner-up for the John Bray Award (South Australian Premier's Award), David Reiter has selected his favourites from his first six collections as well as new work that figures in some of his ground-breaking multimedia. The poems travel from Arctic Canada to contemporary Australia and many points between. Strongly narrative, his work has a wide readership internationally as well as in Australia.

About the Author: Dr David Reiter has been publishing poetry for nearly 25 years and has 14 titles in various genres to his name including poetry, fiction, scripts and multimedia. An academic for many years, he was influenced by the American modernists and post-modernists, and is particularly interested in the place of myth and history in our culture. Several of his books create voices of artists he admires such as van Gogh, Gauguin, and Hemingway. He lives in Brisbane with his wife and two children, where he is Director of IP.

David P Reiter

Link: http://www.ipoz.biz/titles/kt.htm

Title: *Subterranean Radio Songs*
Author: Joel Deane
Publisher/Imprint: IP/Interactive Press
ISBN: 1-876819-31-6 PB, 89 pp. RRP: AU$23
Release Date: 15 October 2005

Description: Winner IP Picks Best Poetry, 2005. *Subterranean Radio Songs* is a collection of poetry that forms a narrative of the author's travels from Australia to the Americas and the Himalayas, with frequent detours into our mind and soul. The collection melds travel with urban life and the trials that we face, brought to life by Joel Deane's vivid language and evocative description.

About the Author: IP Picks Award 2004 winner for his debut novel, *Another*, Joel Deane has had numerous works published, particularly between 1990 and 1995. He fell silent as a writer until 2004, and this collection is the story of those silent years. He currently works as a speechwriter for the Premier of Victoria, Steve Bracks. Joel lives in Melbourne with his wife and two children.

Joel Deane

Link: http://www.ipoz.biz/titles/srs.htm

Title: *Dark Husk of Beauty*
Author: Dr. Andrew Leggett
Publisher/Imprint: IP/Interactive Press
ISBN 10: 1-876819-38-3 • ISBN 13: 9781876819385
PB, 72 pp. RRP: AU$24
Release Date: October, 2006

Description: Commended, Best Poetry, IP Picks 2006. Dark Husk of Beauty explores the duality of beauty and ugliness, of creation and destruction. The title section addresses the disintegrative beauty of the body subject to the ravages of passion, disease and death. The second section takes up the metaphor of "Prophecy" – Ezekiel's prophecy over the plain of dry bones that, gathered together, grow flesh and are restored to life. In the third section, "Wings of Desire", the poems defy aesthetic dualism, undeterred by the punishments inflicted for the artists' heresy. The final poem, a sequence of versions of lesser-known works of Rilke, attempts to negotiate the portal separating such extremes through grace.

About the Author: Andrew Leggett is a Brisbane poet who works as a psychiatrist and psychoanalytic psychotherapist. His work has been widely published in magazines, professional journals, newspapers and anthologies throughout Australia, the UK, the USA and New Zealand. His first collection, *Old Time Religion and Other Poems*, was published by Interactive Press in 1998. The manuscript of his second collection, *Dark Husk of Beauty*, was short-listed in the Arts Queensland Thomas Shapcott Award in 2005, and has formed the main body of his Master of Philosophy dissertation in Creative Writing. He was also a prize winner in the Arts Queensland Val Vallis Award in 2004.

Dr. Andrew Leggett

Link: http://www.ipoz.biz/titles/dhb.htm

Printed in the United Kingdom
by Lightning Source UK Ltd.
120638UK00001B/22